CRAFTING WITH
WOOD PALLETS

CRAFTING WITH
WOOD PALLETS

PROJECTS FOR RUSTIC FURNITURE, DECOR, ART, GIFTS AND MORE

BECKY LAMB

ULYSSES PRESS

Published in the U.S. by
Ulysses Press
P.O. Box 3440
Berkeley, CA 94703
www.ulyssespress.com

ISBN: 978-1-61243-488-9
Library of Congress Control Number: 2015937556

Printed in the United States by Versa Press

20 19 18 17 16 15 14 13 12 11 10 9 8 7

Acquisitions editor: Casie Vogel
Managing editor: Claire Chun
Editor: Susan Lang
Proofreader: Renee Rutledge
Front cover design: Michelle Thompson
Interior design and layout: what!design @ whatweb.com
Index: Sayre Van Young

This book is dedicated to my family, who have lovingly and enthusiastically supported me.
You are the best project and creation in my life.
And to my mom, who inspired me throughout my life
to be an independent and strong woman.

CONTENTS

INTRODUCTION

I was blessed to be raised by a mother who had a do-it-yourself attitude. She decorated our home on a tight budget, often creating the decor she wanted for a few dollars. When my sister and I spied a rainbow bedroom with L-shaped beds and a modular desk set in a catalog, our mom made it for us on limited funds. She painted, sewed, decoupaged, and used a screwdriver to create a beautiful home.

Some of my fondest memories are from when I was allowed to create my own projects. I would decoupage alongside my mom, making "art" from old greeting cards and scraps of wood. I sewed pillows and doll clothes from fabric scraps, and I even built a fort from old grocery store crates that my dad brought home.

Decorating on a budget stayed with me, not only out of necessity but also because I enjoy the challenge of creating a beautiful space for very little money. I like taking something that someone finds useless and turning it into a new, fresh piece. I love being creative and making items for my home that are unique and personal.

My husband helped to further my passion for budget decorating. He is a frugal man who enjoys working with his hands and building. In the beginning of my woodworking career I would ask him to do the cutting, sanding, and drilling for me. That didn't last long because our schedules didn't allow us to work on projects at the same time, and I was often like a toddler, wanting to do it myself. He patiently taught me the safe use of power tools and the correct way to assemble components so that an item was sturdy and well made.

I am not sure when I first saw something made from a shipping pallet, but I do know I was instantly enthralled. I saw the possibilities of an endless supply of free wood. My mind worked overtime thinking of different ways to use pallets. My first project was the simple and popular pallet shelf that I changed a bit by adding coat hooks. That was all it took: I was hooked on pallets and have been imagining the possibilities and creating with them ever since that first pallet shelf.

I began stalking alleys and parts stores for pallets. I hauled them home in my little SUV. Pallets come in all sizes — I currently have a couple of 12-foot-long pallets for a floor in a backyard shed my family and I are building from pallets. I experimented and found the best way to take pallets apart.

I love finding pallets made from all kinds of wood. When I found my first pallet made from solid hickory, my heart skipped a beat because hickory is a hardwood used for fine furniture and cabinet making. And I had found it for free! My family also looks out for pallets and brings them home for me. The joy of finding the perfect pallet still thrills me. My hope is that through reading this book you discover the same joy and love for pallets, that you find your creativity, and that you learn something new you can use always.

This book shares 26 pallet projects that you can make, personalize, and use as a springboard to dream up your own pallet projects. It begins with all of the basics you need to know to get started building with pallets, plus a tutorial on my favorite and most popular painting technique. Once you build one or two of these projects, you will practically be an expert. In the building chapters you will find projects for a range of abilities, from beginner to expert levels, with step-by-step instructions and pictures. The final building chapter shows you what to do with all of those bits and pieces, the scraps you can't bear to throw out. So grab a mug of your favorite beverage, sit back and read, and start planning which pallet projects you will create first!

PALLETS 101: EVERYTHING YOU NEED TO KNOW

FINDING PALLETS

Once I decided I wanted to build with pallets, I needed to find some. One drive around my small town and I discovered plenty of sources of quality pallets: a flooring store, a heating and air conditioning business, a plumbing supply store, a glass shop, and the local newspaper. I always go into the business and ask if pallets are free for the taking. Most often the business is thrilled that someone wants to take pallets off their hands. Also, pallets are often listed in the "free section" of classified ads. Once you find a couple of good sources, you will know where to look for the perfect pallet for a particular project.

WHAT TO LOOK FOR WHEN PICKING PALLETS

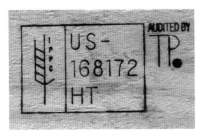

After you discover where to find free pallets, you need to know what to look for because not all pallets are created equal. Most important: Look for the IPPC (International Plant Protection Convention) label or the HT stamp on the pallet.

The IPPC identifier means that the manufacturer has followed the regulated international standard for treating pallets. The HT identifier means that the pallet wood has been heat treated, rather than chemically treated. Do not use a pallet if you do not see the IPPC label or the HT stamp. Pallets that are only for domestic shipping may not have the IPPC label, but you can only be sure they are safe if they have the label. The stamp also shows the pallet's country of origin. The country of origin is not important as long as the pallet has the IPPC label. Most of the pallets I use are from the U.S.; a few are from Canada. In addition, check the pallet for anything that looks like chemical or oil residue. Stay away from any suspect pallets — it is not worth the risk of getting something unknown on your skin or in your lungs. Many pallets have black skid marks on them from transport. These pallets are safe to use, and most often the marks can be easily sanded off.

Next, look for pallets that are solid. Check the individual boards for cracks and splits in the wood. Almost every pallet has one or two unusable boards, so choose pallets that have mostly good boards. Some of the split boards can be glued back together and used. Look at the 2" × 4" support boards — do you need straight boards or notched ones for your project? Choose a pallet with boards in the width required for the project. Also, find pallets made from different types of wood so that you have a variety of wood types for various projects. Lighter pallets are probably made from pine or cedar. Heavier pallets are probably made from harder woods such as oak, hickory, and even cherry. In addition, looking at the wood grain helps to identify the wood type.

TOOLS AND EQUIPMENT

I have collected a nice selection of tools over the years, but I started with the most basic equipment: hammer, saw, drill, and sander. Many of the pallet projects in this book can be built using an inexpensive jigsaw (mine is 20 years old and the most basic version), a small cordless drill, and a palm sander. Nicer, better tools do make the work easier, and I generally find that you get what you pay for. But the best tools aren't necessary to complete these projects. Buy the best tools you can afford, and then upgrade when you are able to. Good used tools are often available at garage sales, pawn shops, and online sale sites.

SAFETY

It is important to use tools safely. Read and follow all safety instructions for the tools you are using. ALWAYS wear safety goggles when using any power tools. Wear gloves, especially to protect against rough wood and slivers.

A respirator mask or a dust mask is important to wear while sanding.

SAWS

A jigsaw or another type of reciprocating saw, such as a Sawzall, are the best tools for taking pallets apart. Saw blades made for cutting metal are necessary for cutting through nails. These blades are usually painted white, blue, or yellow. I recommend a corded saw as opposed to a cordless version. A cordless saw does not have enough power and needs to be recharged often.

A miter saw is the most accurate and quickest way to cut pallet boards to different lengths or to cut angles. You also could use a jigsaw, a circular saw, or a handsaw instead. For cutting angles you can use the power miter saw or a handsaw with an inexpensive miter box.

HAMMER AND MINI CROWBAR

A hammer with a good claw (the forked end used for removing nails) and a mini crowbar are needed to take apart a pallet and to remove nails.

CLAMPS

Clamps in a variety of sizes are invaluable for keeping wood pieces in place when drilling and screwing, and for holding wood together when gluing. They serve as a second pair of "hands."

ELECTRIC SANDER

An electric sander makes the job of sanding rough pallet wood much easier. Palm sanders are small, lightweight, and easy to use. There are different types of electric palm sanders. A random orbit sander has a round sanding pad that spins when sanding, while an orbital sander usually has a square sanding pad that vibrates. You can buy hook and loop sandpaper, adhesive sandpaper, or regular sandpaper that attaches to the sander one quarter of a sheet at a time. Check to see what type of sandpaper your sander uses as all sanders are different. I use a random orbit sander because it works more quickly than an orbital sander. This sander also has a variable speed dial; most orbital sanders do not.

I most often use two different grits of sandpaper. The larger the number on the sandpaper, the finer the grit. For unfinished pallet wood I generally use 60 grit, or coarse, sandpaper because the wood is rough. I use 120 or 150 grit for finish sanding and for sanding paint.

BRAD NAILER OR BRAD GUN

For a few projects I use a brad nailer, or brad gun, to attach wood pieces. I do this when I don't want too many screws showing; for example, when attaching wood pieces for a tabletop. My brad nailer works with an air compressor and uses skinny "nails" or brads. There are some brad nailers that are electric and do not require an air compressor. If you don't have a brad nailer, small finish nails and a hammer can be used. Small finish nails have a little bit larger head than a brad and work equally well, but take more time.

CORDLESS DRILL AND DRILL BITS

A cordless drill is one of those tools you will wonder how you ever got along without. I started with the cheapest one and over the years traded up. You want a drill that has at least a 12-volt battery; mine has an 18-volt. I now own two drills. I keep a drill bit to drill holes on one drill and a Phillips head screw bit on the other. I like using smaller, lightweight drills as long as they have a decent-size battery.

In addition to a cordless drill, you also need a set of drill bits. I usually buy extra drill bits in the sizes I use the most (for example, size $\frac{3}{32}$") because sometimes they break off. I typically pre-drill all holes before adding screws so that the pallet wood does not split when screwing in the screw.

SCREWS

You'll need a variety of screws for the projects in this book. I buy screws in bulk, paying by the pound, at my local hardware store. I sort the screws by size and keep them in empty nut and candy containers, and I write the screw size on the lid.

TAPE MEASURE

A tape measure is essential. I have a couple: I keep one by my saw and one in my toolbox.

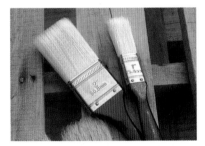

PAINTBRUSHES

I mostly use brushes called chip brushes or natural bristle brushes. They are inexpensive and leave a rougher finish, which I like on pallet wood. I prefer nylon bristle brushes, which leave fewer brush marks, for use with chalkboard paint.

PICTURE-HANGING HARDWARE

Many of the projects in this book require picture-hanging hardware. For an item that is heavy or might become off-balance when something is placed on it (like a coat hook), I use ½" D rings on the back. D rings come with their own screws to secure them to the project. I hang other items with 40-pound picture hanging wire and screws (usually ¾" or 1").

TAKING APART PALLETS

Taking apart pallets does require some time and work. The job is easier with two people, but I have taken apart many pallets by myself. Please use extra caution when disassembling pallets: Always wear protective eyewear, long pants, and close-toed shoes. Be conscious of where your saw cord is while cutting so that you do not nick it or cut through it.

The quickest and easiest way to cut wood off a pallet is to use a reciprocating saw, such as a Sawzall, with a blade for cutting metal. The long blade easily slips between the pallet wood pieces to cut the nails holding them together. Have someone hold the pallet for you or steady the pallet by keeping your foot on the bottom board while you cut. This method will leave nail parts in the wood, especially in the 2" × 4" pieces. A handheld jigsaw fitted with a metal blade will also take apart a pallet, although the jigsaw blade is not as long as the blade on a Sawzall type of reciprocating saw.

USING A RECIPROCATING SAW

A mini crowbar and a hammer provide another way to remove pallet boards. This method is more work, but I often use it when removing just one or two boards or when I want to remove all of the nails from the boards. Hammer the mini crowbar in between the pallet boards to wedge them apart and loosen the nail heads. Use the hammer claw to pull out the nails.

USING A MINI CROWBAR AND HAMMER

To cut pallet parts from a pallet without completely removing the boards, use a handheld jigsaw or circular saw.

A reciprocating saw like a Sawzall can also be used to cut pallet wood, but the cut usually isn't as accurate or straight.

If a board is unusable, I put it in the burn pile for our fire pit. Some split boards can be clamped and repaired with wood glue. Be sure to get the glue into the crack or split and clamp tightly. Remove any excess glue with a rag or paper towel before it dries. Let the glue dry for 24 hours before unclamping and using the board.

After you take apart a couple of pallets and learn what works best, the job will become easier. I usually disassemble five or more pallets at a time, and it takes me approximately 30 to 45 minutes to take apart five pallets with a reciprocating saw like a Sawzall.

PALLET PARTS

The following photos will help you identify the different parts of a pallet.

BACK SUPPORT OR CROSS PALLET BOARD
MIDDLE 2" X 4" PALLET BOARD
PALLET 2" X 4"

I refer to the main support boards as 2" × 4" boards. Although they are often a bit smaller than typical 2" × 4" boards, in this book, they are called 2" × 4"s for easy reference.

NOTCHED PALLET 2" X 4"

PALLET SIZES

Pallets come in a wide variety of sizes. I have used pallets that are as small as 12" × 24" and ones that are as large as 48" × 120". Smaller-sized pallets most often tend to be 24" × 36" or 36" × 36", while larger-sized pallets are usually 40" × 48" or 48" × 48". I list sizes of pallets I used for the projects in the book, but you will need to be flexible and adjust measurements according to the size of the pallet you are using if you cannot find one in the same size.

PALLET ENDS

A few of the projects in this book refer to a "pallet end" as a part of the supply list. After you make a few projects, you may have some of these lying around as leftovers. But if you don't you can easily cut one from your standard pallet.

INSTRUCTIONS

Use a pencil to mark the outside support 2" × 4" at desired length. This can be any length you choose, depending on the project you're making. You will need to cut through the 2" × 4" outside support boards and the middle support board. The middle board may be a little more challenging, and you may have to cut through from both the top and the bottom.

Pallet ends are great for making small and easy projects. One of my favorites is the Coat Hook and Shelf (page 18). The finished project is a good example of what a simple pallet end, once cut, looks like.

ADDING COLOR: PAINTING TECHNIQUE

I love paint. It transforms objects inexpensively, adds color, is easy to change, and is fun to play with. Over the years, I have experimented with many different painting techniques and ideas. I discovered that pallet wood is the perfect canvas for paint. My technique produces a weathered finish that appears to have been painted several times over many years. Personalize my technique to fit your needs, using the colors that you like to decorate with and enjoy.

SUPPLIES

Paint in a variety of colors ranging from light to dark. I mostly use different brands of interior latex in an eggshell finish. Latex paint, which is a water-based paint that cleans up with water, comes in five finishes: flat, eggshell, satin, semi-gloss, and gloss. Flat paint has no sheen and stains easily, while gloss paint produces the shiniest finish. I like the eggshell finish because it has a little sheen without being too glossy. Also, the glossier the paint is, the more it will "gum up" your sandpaper. I use a white semi-gloss paint for lettering signs because the stain I use to weather the wood will not stick to the semi-gloss paint and therefore, the white stays white. You can also use a gloss paint.

Another type of paint that I like to use is mineral paint made by Fusion Mineral Paint (see sources at end of book). This paint has great coverage, dries quickly, and sticks well to many different types of surfaces.

There are a few times in the book where I use craft paint rather than latex. I use this when I need only a small amount of paint in a certain color.

- Paint
- Electric sander or sandpaper (For hand sanding, use 120 or 150 grit, depending on how much paint you want removed.)
- 3 or 4 paintbrushes, 1½" wide
- Stain (I most often use the color Early American.)
- Clear finish
- Rags (old T-shirts)
- Gloves

TECHNIQUE

1 Paint several pallet boards at once for current and future projects. Lay a variety of pallet boards on a drop cloth or a piece of cardboard. If you want more of the wood to show through the paint, do not sand the boards before painting. If you want the boards to be mostly all painted, sand the wood before painting.

2 I use three brushes, usually inexpensive chip brushes or natural hair brushes. I always keep at least one paintbrush for painting with red paint only. It is difficult to remove all of the red paint from the brush and it will taint other colors.

3 Start by painting with the lightest colors. Here I started with golden yellow and moss green. Do not paint every board. On the boards you paint, do not completely cover the wood with paint. This allows more colors to come through the paint layers. By the end, some boards will have three or four colors on them, some only two. I do not clean my paint brushes between colors. I do try to "paint off" most of the color from the brush before changing colors.

4 When the paint is mostly dry, paint the next lightest colors, such as bright green and light blue. Do not completely cover the previous colors.

5 Continue with your paint colors, applying the darker colors over the lighter ones.

6 When the paint is fairly dry, use the lightest colors again to paint a few of the boards. This creates a handful of boards with light colors on the top layer, for variety.

7 Clean the paintbrushes with warm water and a small amount of liquid dish soap.

8 When the paint is dry, sand the boards with 120 or 150 grit sandpaper. Use the 120 grit if you want to remove more paint, 150 grit if you want the paint removal to be a little more subtle. The paint will come off easily from the rough areas of the pallet wood. Sanding will reveal the colors under the top paint color. Some exposed wood with no paint on it is desirable.

9 Next, apply stain over the painted boards, and be sure to wear gloves to protect your hands. Use a chip brush reserved for stain, and completely cover the paint. Wipe the excess stain off with a rag, and properly dispose of used rags according to the stain manufacturer's directions.

10 Wait to apply a clear finish until you use the boards in a project. The type of project will determine the finish. The type of clear finish that I use most often is an acrylic spray-on sealer made for both indoor and outdoor use. I also use a brush-on polyacrylic, which creates a thicker protective finish than the spray-on sealer. Be watchful for drips with a brush-on finish. In addition, I like coconut oil (used frequently in cooking) as a finish, especially over unpainted wood. It is all-natural, does not get rancid, and brings out the wood's natural colors. It should not be used on outdoor pieces. Coconut oil does provide a protective finish, but not as strong as the acrylic sealers do.

STORAGE AND ORGANIZATION

COAT HOOK AND SHELF

This project holds a special place in my heart. It is the first pallet project I ever created, and so I chose to put it first in this book. An easy project, it requires the end of a pallet and a 2" × 4" board. It is one of those versatile pieces that works in just about every room of the house — and also makes a wonderful housewarming gift for someone special.

SUPPLIES

- One notched pallet end (I used a 36"-wide pallet end.)
- One 2"× 4" pallet support board

- Three coat hooks
- 1⅝" screws
- ¾" screws
- Paint

- Stain or clear finish
- Paintbrush
- D rings

TOOLS

- Saw
- Palm sander

- Drill
- Tape measure

TIME: 1 hour, plus dry time   LEVEL: Beginner

1 Measure each side of the open end of the pallet. Be sure to measure each side, as the sides often are different lengths. For example, mine were 15¼" wide and 15¾" long. From the 2" × 4" board, cut two pieces the lengths you measured.

2 Sand the boards and the pallet end. Sand the inside of the pallet end by hand.

3 Fit the 2" × 4" boards over the bottom of the pallet end. Use four 1⅝" screws to secure each 2" x 4" to the pallet end to create the bottom shelf, drilling two screws in through the front of the pallet end and two from the back.

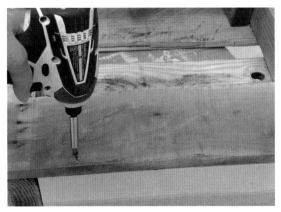

4 Attach coat hooks to the front of the shelf with ¾" screws. Because I wanted to paint the coat hooks, I added them before painting the shelf. If you are not painting the hooks, wait and add them after painting the shelf.

5 Finish as desired using paint, stain, or simply a clear finish on the pallet wood. Attach D rings on the back to hang the shelf.

PALLET POINTERS: STORAGE IDEAS

In the kitchen, this shelf can hold cookbooks, spices, oils, aprons, and towels.

Hang two or three of these shelves low in a child's room for book storage. Hooks are easy for even the smallest of children to use.

Place this shelf in the mudroom for cleaning supplies. Hang cleaning cloths, mops, and brooms from the hooks.

Use the shelf outside on the garden shed or attached to a fence for garden tools. Be sure to seal the wood if using outdoors.

A GREAT CRATE

I love a great crate, and I always have. As I mentioned in the introduction, I even once built a fort out of old fruit crates from the grocery store. But old crates are hard to find, often rickety, and not very useful for holding much of anything. No worries — now you can make your own sturdy crate in any size you want from pallet pieces.

This great crate is a true workhorse in the home. Use several to keep kids' toys organized or to store hats and mittens in the mudroom. I utilize mine for books and magazines, blankets and towels, and paint and craft supplies. I keep some in my pantry to store canned pickles and applesauce. The possibilities are endless!

SUPPLIES

- Four 5½" × 18" pallet boards
- Two 5½" × 10" pallet boards
- 1⅝" screws
- ½" screws
- 2 handles (I used 6" pieces from an old leather belt.)
- Paint
- Stain
- Paintbrushes

- Palm sander
- Drill
- Tape measure
- Clamp

TIME: 1 hour, plus dry time   LEVEL: Beginner

1 You'll use the four 5½" × 18" boards for the long sides and bottom of the crate, and the two 5½" × 10" boards for the short sides of the crate. Set the two long sides on edge, and rest one bottom board on them (or clamp the boards to keep them stable).

2 Attach the bottom board to one of the long sides with 1⅝" screws. Move the unsecured long side farther out, and set the other bottom board on top. Attach that bottom board to the long side with 1⅝" screws. You will have two L-shaped pieces because the bottom pieces are not yet connected.

3 Join the bottom boards together by installing the short sides of the crate. Insert 1⅝" screws into the short sides from the crate bottom. Notice how warped the long side pieces are. Pallets aren't always perfect and you can work with warped wood if necessary.

4 Clamp the sides of the crate, and insert two 1⅝" screws through each end of the long sides into the short sides.

5 Sand the crate. I like to round the sharp edges — this helps to even out the crate sides and create a worn look, as if the crate has been around for years.

6 Paint and stain as desired.

7 Add handles. I used leather belt pieces cut with a utility or craft knife and secured with ½" screws. You want screws the same thickness as the pallet wood so they do not show on the inside of the crate. I find that the screws will be more secure and tighter if you just start to pre-drill the screw holes but don't completely drill them.

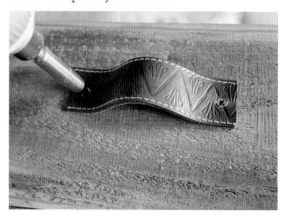

PALLET POINTERS: HANDLES

You can use many different things as handles: leather belts, wood blocks or scraps from a 2" × 4" board, bent silverware, kitchen cabinet handles, odd pieces of rusty junk, old tools with wood handles, thick pieces of branch, rope, or canvas fabric strips — use your imagination!

Secure the handles well so they stay put even when you carry something heavy in the crate.

CATCH-ALL CADDY

I like "stuff" and always have been a collector and saver of more things than I need. But although I tend to have clutter, I do like to keep my stuff corralled and somewhat organized in various containers and boxes. This catch-all caddy is perfect for doing just that. I can think of a hundred different places and ways to use this fun piece. Not only is it a great place to organize belongings, but it looks fantastic too.

SUPPLIES

- Two pallet ends (This one measures 10" wide × 18" long.)
- One 3½"-wide pallet board, at least ½" thick and 36" long
- 1¼" screws
- 2" screws
- Paintbrushes
- Clear sealer
- Painter's tape
- Chalkboard paint
- Chalk
- Handle of choice

TOOLS

- Saw
- Palm sander
- Drill
- Tape measure

TIME: 1½ hours, plus dry time   LEVEL: Beginner

1 Find a pallet that has two similar-looking ends that are in decent condition. My two pieces are 18" long.

2 Place the pallet ends back to back so that the taller sections touch. Join them with two 1¼" screws inserted through one top piece into the other top piece.

3 Join the bottom pieces of the caddy with three 1¼" screws through one side into the other side.

4 Measure the length of the opening at the bottom of each pallet piece. My pallet opening measures 15" long. Be sure to measure each opening as they may be a little different.

5 Cut the 3½"-wide pallet board into the two lengths you measured. Mine were each 15" long. Secure those pieces to the bottom of the caddy with two 2" screws on each end.

7 Add a handle. I used a piece of a leather belt screwed into the top with 1¼" screws. See Pallet Pointers: Handles on page 23 for other handle ideas.

6 Sand well, then brush on clear sealer. When the sealer is dry, tape off the edges of the two long side panels and paint with chalkboard paint, let dry, and season the chalkboard. See Pallet Pointers: Chalkboard Paint on page 31 for details.

PALLET POINTERS: USES

This caddy is perfect for outdoor dining, or keep it in the kitchen to hold dishtowels and the spices and condiments you use most often.

You could use the caddy in a craft room for scissors and punches, and paper and paint. It will hold a whole mess of children's art supplies. Or keep it in the garage to hold tools. How about putting it to work in the bathroom holding toiletries and washcloths or in the family room for magazines and books? Once you discover how handy and useful this caddy is, you will want to make several.

COMMAND CENTRAL

If you are like me and your life is busy, you'll appreciate anything to help you organize yourself and your family. This command central message board is the perfect place to keep everything important. It has a chalkboard for messages and lists, hooks for keys, binder clips for coupons, and slots for mail, magazines, and newspapers. Hang it above a desk or in the kitchen or mudroom — wherever your family will see it on a daily basis.

SUPPLIES

- One small pallet (mine is 26" x 31") with a solid top (a top with no spaces between the pallet boards)
- Two 5½" × 26" pallet boards
- Three metal cup hooks
- Two large binder clips
- D rings
- 1½" screws
- 1" screws
- Painter's tape
- Chalkboard paint
- Paint in various colors
- Paintbrushes
- Stain
- Chalk

TOOLS

- Saw
- Palm sander
- Drill
- Tape measure

TIME: 1 hour, plus dry time   LEVEL: Beginner

1 Remove the top and middle back cross boards from the small pallet.

2 Sand the solid interior surface of the pallet, and cover with chalkboard paint.

3 Paint the edges and sides of the pallet in the desired colors. I used red, green, and turquoise. I did not paint the insides of the support boards because I wanted a natural wood finish somewhere on the message board.

4 Using 1½" screws, attach the 5½" × 26" boards to the top and the bottom of the pallet. The overhang at the bottom makes an ideal ledge for holding chalk.

5 Tape off the painted chalkboard, and stain the rest of the message center, being careful not to get any stain on the chalkboard. Use a clear brush on polyacrylic over the areas you stained, again being careful not to get the sealer on the chalkboard paint.

6 Add cup hooks to one side for keys. Pre-drill small holes for screwing in the hooks.

7 Using 1" screws, add binder clips to the other side. I rusted the metal clips for a vintage look.

8 Fasten D rings on the back for hanging the message center.

RUSTING METAL ITEMS

To rust metal items, place them in a disposable plastic container and add 2 parts white vinegar to 1 part hydrogen peroxide, and approximately ¼ cup salt. Let the metal items sit in the solution for 24 hours, and then air-dry them on a paper towel. For more rust, sprinkle extra salt on the items as they dry. Note: Some metals such as stainless steel will not rust.

PALLET POINTERS: CHALKBOARD PAINT

Chalkboard paint, in spray and brush-on forms, is sold in hardware stores and craft stores. I always use the brush-on form.

Use a fine bristle brush that will not leave as many brush marks. A nylon bristle brush works well.

Apply two or three thin coats of chalkboard paint rather than one heavy coat.

When the paint is thoroughly dry (I usually allow 24 hours), season the chalkboard. Rub chalk all over the chalkboard, then wipe it off with a dry cloth.

JEWELRY ORGANIZER

Oh, how I love pretty jewelry. I love all the different styles of jewelry, love the colors, love the simple pieces, and love the sentimental pieces like my grandmother's favorite necklace. The part I haven't loved is the storing of it all. I have tried jewelry boxes, wall hooks, a cake stand, and even a CD holder. This simple jewelry organizer works perfectly for me. It's a great place for earrings, bracelets (my favorite pieces), necklaces, and even rings.

SUPPLIES

- One pallet end (This one measures 20½" wide × 13¼" tall.)
- One 2" × 4" pallet support board, cut 20½" long
- 1⅝" screws
- ½" screw eyes
- ⅜" wood dowel, cut into three 4" lengths
- Wood glue
- Paint
- Paintbrushes
- 18 gauge wire
- D rings

TOOLS

- Palm sander
- Drill
- Tape measure
- Pencil

TIME: 1 hour, plus dry time **LEVEL:** Intermediate

1 Find a pallet end or cut a scrap piece from a larger pallet (page 12) that looks similar to this. Pallet ends are unique and may look different from my photos here. This is half or only one side of a pallet end. (The 2" × 4" board cut to required length is also shown in picture.)

2 Attach the 2" × 4" pallet board to the bottom of the pallet section with 1⅝" screws.

3 Measure and mark the center of the 2" × 4" board, and mark 5" away from the center mark on either side.

4 Using an $^{11}/_{32}$" drill bit (one size smaller than the $^3/_8$" dowel), drill a hole in each place you marked. Set a piece of scrap wood under the 2" × 4" board, and drill all the way through the board. You may need to reach down through the pallet slats to drill.

5 Put wood glue in the holes, and insert a dowel in each hole. You may need to gently hammer to get the dowels all the way into the holes.

6 When the glue is dry, sand and paint the jewelry organizer as desired. I used three colors: yellow, light mossy green, and ocean blue.

7 After the paint is dry, drill a hole in the center of each of the pallet side boards on the inside of the jewelry organizer, 1" down from the top. Screw in the screw eyes, but not tightly.

8 Cut a 22" length of wire and secure it around the screw eyes. Tighten the screw eyes to tighten the wire. This creates hanging storage for jewelry like earrings.

9 Attach D rings on the back for hanging.

DOUBLE-DECKER STORAGE BINS

This is one of those projects you'll want to repeat. Once you make these storage bins, you will want to make more because they are so useful. They're handy in just about every room in the house — in an entryway for mittens and shoes, in the kitchen for potatoes, in the bathroom for towels and toilet paper, and in the playroom for toys and books. Wherever you put the bins, you will love how much they hold and how useful they are.

SUPPLIES

- Four 3½" × 39½" pallet boards, ¾" thick
- Eight 5½" × 17" pallet boards cut at a 45-degree angle at one end (long side 17" long, short side 12" long)
- Ten 3½" × 18" pallet boards
- Four 5½" × 19½" pallet boards
- Scrap piece of pallet board 4¾" wide to use as spacer
- 1" screws
- Paint
- Stain
- Paintbrushes

TOOLS

- Miter saw or miter box
- Palm sander
- Drill
- Tape measure
- Clamp

TIME: 2 hours, plus dry time   LEVEL: Intermediate

1 Cut all of the pallet boards to the sizes listed above, and sand them.

2 Lay out two of the 39½" boards (the legs), using the scrap piece of pallet as a spacer in between to keep the boards equal distance apart. Place two of the angled boards at the top of the legs so that they form a point aimed toward you, placing the top angled board flush with the top of the legs.

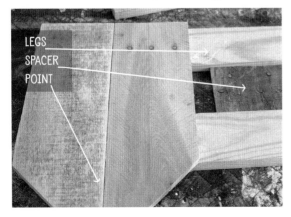

3 Screw the angled boards to the legs.

4 Measure and mark 11¼" down from the bottom angled board. Place two more angled boards on the legs in a point facing you, and attach them as you did the top two angled boards.

5 Repeat steps 2 to 4 to make the second side piece, but place the two points so they face away from you while building. This creates an opposite side, so that the legs and sides will end up on the outside of the bins.

6 Use three of the 3½" × 18" pallet boards to make the bottom of each of the two bins. Screw the boards into the bottom angled pieces, spacing them equally apart. Your storage bins will look like this.

7 Attach two 5½" × 19½" boards to the back of each bin, using a clamp to hold the boards in place. Screw the back boards into the leg boards, not the angled boards.

8 Screw two 3½" × 18" boards to the bottom angled boards at the front of each bin. Use a clamp to hold the boards in place.

9 Paint and stain as desired. I painted the outside red, left the inside natural, and then stained the whole piece.

PALLET POINTERS: VERSATILE STORAGE

Use shorter, narrower boards to make a smaller version of the storage bins.

You can make the bins wider to hold even more stuff.

Chalkboard paint painted on the front of the bins will help everyone know what belongs in the bins.

RECORD SHELF CRATE

Crates are so wonderfully versatile and useful. This crate is larger than the Great Crate (page 21). Make two or three and stack them on their side to create a fantastic shelf, perfect for all of your vintage vinyl, books, and magazines. The stackable crates also work as a useful side table next to a favorite chair.

SUPPLIES

- Four 5½" × 42" pallet boards, ⅝" thick
- One 5½" × 42" pallet board, ¼"–½" thick
- Two 3½" pallet boards that are at least 24" long
- 1⅝" screws
- 1¼" screws
- Clear sealer
- Paintbrush

TOOLS

- Saw
- Palm sander
- Drill
- Tape measure
- Clamp

TIME: 1½ hours   LEVEL: Intermediate

1 For the sides of the crate, cut two of the thicker 42"-long boards into four pieces, each 20" long. For the bottom of the crate, cut the thinner 42"-long board into two pieces, each 20" long.

2 Cut the two remaining thicker 42"-long boards into four pieces, each 12" long for the crate ends.

3 Cut the 3½"-wide boards into four pieces, each 12" long. Sand all of the boards well before assembly.

4 Attach each of the two thinner 20" bottom boards to one of the thicker 20" side boards. Insert 1⅝" screws through the bottom board into the bottom edge of the side board. You will have two L-shaped pieces.

5 Use the 3½" × 12" pieces to add the second 20"-long side piece to the L-shaped piece you created. Secure the 12" pieces with 1⅝" screws, inserted into the ends of the 20" boards. There will be about a 1" space between the two side boards.

6 Next, create the crate ends (the short sides of the crate). Using one 1¼" screw, attach one of the 5½" × 12" pallet boards to the bottom end of the crate side, placing the end board perpendicular to the crate side. Insert the screw through the front of the 3½"-wide vertical support board (i.e., through the outside of the crate rather than from the inside of the crate).

7 Using one 1¼" screw, screw through the crate bottom board into the bottom edge of the 5½" × 12" crate ends. Repeat steps six and seven for the other crate end.

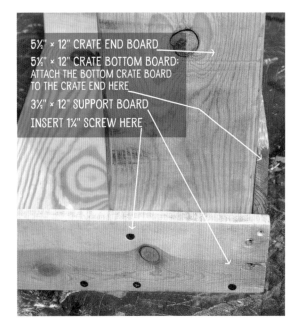

8 Use a large clamp to hold the top crate end board (the 5½" × 12" board) in place, and secure it to the 3½" × 12" vertical support board with two 1¼" screws, again screwing through the front of the 3½"-wide board or through the outside of the crate rather than the inside.

9 Finish as desired. I chose to keep the crate its natural light color and use a clear sealer to protect the wood.

PALLET POINTERS: MIX AND MATCH

For a more secure crate shelf, screw separate crates together to form the shelf.

Make the crates different sizes and stack several together to make a unique entertainment center. Be sure to secure the crates to each other with screws.

Make three crates and paint them bright colors for a fun shelf in a kid's room. Be sure to secure the stacked crates to each other with screws.

Make two much larger crates by keeping the side boards the original pallet board size, usually 40" long. Place the two crates back to back to create a coffee table with lots of storage.

AROUND THE HOUSE

SOFA ARM DESK

This project was born out of necessity. When we bought a new recliner sofa, we realized that the coffee table wasn't going to work anymore. But where was I going to put my coffee, my computer, and my reading glasses? I have space for only one end table next to the sofa. I decided to build a sturdy "desk" or table that rested on the arm of the new sofa and had a space to hold my laptop, which is often in our family room. The desk works great and most often stays on the sofa arm. It also works well sitting on the middle cushion of the sofa when it's vacant. When we do want to stretch out, we store the desk under the end table.

SUPPLIES
- Six 5½"-wide pallet boards, at least 24" long
- Two 2" × 4" pallet boards, cut 16½" long
- 1¼" screws
- Paint
- Clear finish
- Paintbrush

TOOLS
- Saw
- Palm sander
- Drill
- Tape measure

1 Measure the width of the arm on your sofa. You want the desk to sit snugly on the arm. From 5½"-wide pallet boards, cut six pieces the width of the arm. For example, the arm on my sofa measures 13" wide, so I cut six 5½"-wide pallet boards 13" long.

2 Cut six 5½"-wide pallet boards 9" long. If you have a particularly tall sofa arm, you will want to make the sofa desk taller than 9", but 9" tall will work for most sofas. After cutting the pallet pieces, sand them well since the desk will be sitting on fabric.

3 To make the top of the sofa arm desk, place three of the 13" (or the size you cut) boards on top of the two 2" × 4" pieces, and secure them with 1¼" screws.

4 Turn the desk over and do the same with the remaining 13" boards to create a cubby for books and magazines.

5 Place three of the 9" pallet boards across the 2" x 4". Secure each 9" board to the 2" x 4" with two 1¼" screws per board. Place screws at an angle. Repeat on the other side of the desk. These create the sides that help to keep the desk securely sitting on the sofa arm.

6 Paint and finish as desired. I painted the outside and left the inside the natural, light color of the pallet wood.

TOWEL HOLDER

We have a nice master bathroom, but it lacks a linen closet. For years we have stored extra towels under the bathroom sink with, well, just about everything else. I finally decided we needed a place for the towels, and this pallet project was the perfect solution. It has room for towels as well as toiletries. Even kids can hang a towel on a hook. This is a quick and easy project, using only one whole pallet and a couple of other pieces.

SUPPLIES
- One small pallet (The one shown here measures 20" × 32".)
- One 2" × 4" pallet support piece
- 2" screws
- Two to four coat hooks
- D rings
- Paint
- Paintbrush
- Clear sealer

TOOLS
- Saw
- Palm sander
- Drill
- Tape measure

1 Start with a small pallet. Make sure it has sturdy cross pieces on the underside because you will be attaching hooks to one of these supports.

2 Measure the length of each side from the inside side piece to the middle cross piece. Be sure to measure each side because often the middle cross piece is not exactly in the center. Also measure the width of the side pieces.

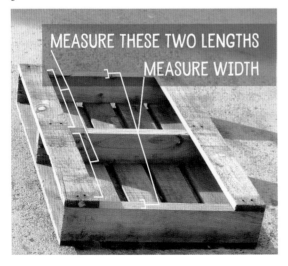

MEASURE THESE TWO LENGTHS
MEASURE WIDTH

3 Based on your measurements, cut two boards from a pallet 2" × 4" board to use as the cubby shelf bottoms. My 2" × 4" boards were cut 15" long. Sand these boards and the pallet.

4 Place the cubby shelf bottoms in place, and attach them through the back (the side with the pallet slats and not the open side). Use two 2" screws for each shelf bottom.

5 Insert one more screw through each side to the shelf bottom. You do not need to use any screws from the front because the shelf bottoms should be very sturdy.

6 Paint in the desired color. Don't bother painting the back. Why waste the time or paint when the back will sit against a wall? When the towel holder is dry, seal it well with a clear spray since it will be used in a bathroom.

7 When the paint is dry, attach up to four hooks for towels onto the bottom cross board. Measure to evenly place the hooks.

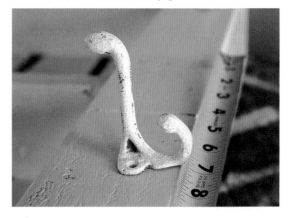

8 Use ½" D rings on the back to hang the towel holder.

Bath towels folded in quarters and then rolled up fit snuggly in the shelf for storage. The upper shelf is a great place for extra toiletries, washcloths, and hand towels.

If you don't need extra storage space in your bathroom, this piece works well in other areas of your home. Use it in a mudroom for storing your iron, cleaning supplies, and towels, and for hanging shirts and clothes that need ironing. Or hang the shelf on a fence next to the pool or hot tub for towels, wet bathing suits, and pool chemicals.

PALLET POINTERS: HOOKS

Purchase hooks at hardware stores, craft stores, or online sites.

Many things can be used as hooks: bent silverware, wood sewing spools, wood blocks, drawer knobs, garden hand tools, wood dowels, and spindles.

Be sure the hooks are properly sealed since they will be holding wet towels. Spray with a clear sealer before installing.

COFFEE TABLE

A coffee crate–inspired coffee table is the perfect addition to any family room. This one is easy to build and sturdy enough to dance on (yes, I tried it!). Simple stenciling positioned off-center makes the table look like it was created from a large coffee crate. The natural-colored pallet wood adds to the authentic crate appearance.

SUPPLIES

- One pallet with a solid top (This pallet is 26" x 33".)
- Two 3½" × 26" pallet boards
- Four 2" × 4" pallet boards cut 16" long
- 2" screws
- Stencils of your choice, 2 different fonts
- Chalk
- Craft paint
- Stencil brush
- Coconut oil
- T-shirt rags

TOOLS

- Saw
- Palm sander
- Drill
- Tape measure
- Clamp

1 Remove all of the bottom support boards from the solid topped pallet.

REMOVE ALL BOTTOM SUPPORT BOARDS

2 Using 2" screws, attach the 26"-long pallet boards to the two open ends of the pallet. The 26"-long boards may not be quite wide enough to cover the pallet 2" × 4" boards that are at the end of the pallet. That is okay because this is a rustic piece. Sand the 2" × 4" pallet ends to round the sharp edges at the corners.

3 Attach the 16"-long 2" × 4" legs. With a small clamp holding the leg in place, secure the leg with four 2" screws, two on each side of the leg. Insert the screws into the table side and the leg at an angle rather than in a vertical line on the long side of the pallet table. This makes the leg more stable.

4 Sand the whole table, including the legs.

5 Use a stencil to create your desired design. A chalk line will keep the letters lined up. Because I wanted the tabletop to look like part of a crate, I ran the word "coffee" off the edge. To properly place the stenciling, I started at the end of the word and worked backward. Then I used dark brown craft paint to fill in the stenciled letters.

6 To make sure the word "roasted" was centered properly above the word "coffee," I lightly chalked in the letters with my stencil before painting.

7 Stencil a number in the upper corner, running it perpendicular to the lettering. When the paint is dry, lightly sand the lettering by hand to give it a weathered look.

8 To preserve the natural wood color of the pallet, finish the table with coconut oil applied with a T-shirt rag. After 24 hours, buff the table with a clean, dry T-shirt rag.

PALLET POINTERS: STENCILING TIPS

Purchase a variety of stencils at craft stores. Plastic stencils last longer than cardstock types.

Draw a chalk line to ensure stencils are placed evenly.

Use a stencil brush (a flat bristle, blunt brush).

Hold your brush straight up and down, and dab the paint on the stencil.

Let each letter dry for a minute or two before stenciling the next one.

If you are using the same letter over, make sure it does not have paint on the back before reusing it.

Let the paint sit on a plate for 15 minutes or longer so it thickens a bit before stenciling.

Sand away any areas where the paint bled under the stencil.

ENTRY OR SOFA TABLE

This narrow table is ideal for an entryway or behind a sofa. Because I have a reclining sofa that needs space to tilt back, I use this table in my entryway. It also works great as a sideboard in a dining room, or as a table under a window or in a long hallway. The bottom shelf is perfect for baskets, books, or knickknacks you want to show off. And the fun colors are sure to brighten any area of your home.

SUPPLIES

- Four 5½" × 28" heavy, sturdy pallet boards
- Four 3½" × 11" pallet boards
- Two 3½" × 40" pallet boards
- Three 3½" × 26" pallet boards
- Several pallet boards in various widths but the same thickness, cut 12½" long
- 1¼" screws
- 1⅝" screws
- 1⅜" brads
- Paint in various colors
- Clear brush-on polyacrylic
- Stain
- Paintbrushes

TOOLS

- Saw
- Palm sander
- Drill
- Brad nailer
- Tape measure
- Pencil
- Clamp, if needed

TIME: 1½ hours, plus dry time   LEVEL: Intermediate

1 Cut and lightly sand the pallet pieces.

2 To create the table legs, line up two of the 28"-long boards for each side. Secure each of the two sets of boards at the top with an 11" board and 1¼" screws.

3 Flip each table leg over, measure 6½" from the bottom, and mark.

4 For each table leg, place the top edge of an 11" board on the 6½" mark, and attach with 1¼" screws. These boards will form the brace for the bottom shelf.

5 With the 40"-long boards on their edges, measure and mark 5¼" from each end.

6 Place the table legs on their edges, with the bottom shelf braces toward the inside of the table. Lay each 40"-long board across the top edge of a table side, placing the pencil marks on the outside edge of the top 11" brace board. Secure with 1⅝" screws. This will form the table apron or the table edge that the table top rests on.

7 Next, add the bottom shelf. Evenly space the three 26"-long boards on the bottom brackets, and secure both ends of each board with two 1¼" screws. If necessary, use a clamp to hold the boards in place.

8 Lay the 12½" boards across the top, adjusting wider and narrower pieces as needed to get the correct fit. Once I had the pieces I needed, I painted them before securing them to the table. I also painted the table base and bottom shelf at this time.

9 When the top pieces are dry, secure them to the table apron pieces with a brad nailer. Lift up one board ahead of the one you are nailing so you can see where to nail. Instead of using a brad nail, you could use screws or small finishing nails and a hammer instead.

10 Secure the two end tabletop boards with 1¼" screws because you will hold these boards when moving the table.

11 Sand the paint lightly. Because I wanted to stain the colored paint but leave the white bright white, I applied a brush-on clear polyacrylic finish over the white paint. When the clear coat was thoroughly dry, I stained the colored boards. I used the brush-on polyacrylic over the stain when it was dry to further protect the table.

STEP STOOL

Need a step up? Want to reach the top back corner of that cupboard? Have a wee one who needs a boost to reach the bathroom sink for teeth brushing? Or how about a place to sit to put on your shoes or a small surface to set a few books? This sturdy step stool is just the ticket, and once you see how easy it is to create, you will want to make one for every room of the house.

SUPPLIES

- Three sturdy 3½"-wide pallet boards, at least 32" long
- One 2" × 4" pallet board, at least 46" long
- 2" screws
- 1⅝" screws
- Paint in various colors
- Paintbrushes
- Coconut oil
- T-shirt rags

TOOLS

- Saw
- Palm sander
- Drill
- Tape measure
- Clamp

TIME: 1½ hours, plus dry time   LEVEL: Intermediate

1 Start with sturdy, as-straight-as-possible boards removed from a pallet.

2 Cut three 16" pieces from the pallet boards for the stool top and two 15" pieces for the long sides of the stool apron.

3 Measure the width of the stool top (the three 16" boards placed together).

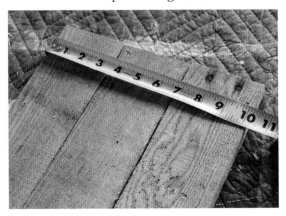

4 Subtract 1" from this measurement. Next, measure the thickness of the two long apron pieces stacked together, and subtract this amount as well. For example, the width of my stool top was 10¼". I subtracted 1", which gave me 9¼", and then subtracted the apron thickness measurement, 1¼", which gave me 8". Cut two pieces this length from the same boards used for the top. These are for the short sides of the stool apron.

5 Cut four 11" legs from the 2" × 4" pallet support board. Secure the short ends of the stool apron to the legs with two 2" screws on each side.

6 Add the long apron pieces the same way, using a clamp to help square the base and hold the pieces in place.

7 Place the stool top boards on the apron. I eyeball the placement to make sure it is even. Secure the boards by inserting $1\frac{5}{8}$" screws through the top of each board into the apron. Lift up the board ahead of the one you are attaching so you can see where to drill.

8 Sand and paint as desired. I painted the top of the stool in three colors, and then rubbed in coconut oil on the apron and legs and over the paint. I purposely left the pallet stamp on the leg because I like the way it looks.

PALLET POINTERS: STOOL VARIATIONS

Make a shorter stool, with 8" legs (instead of 11"), for young children.

Use this same method of building with full-sized pallet boards to make an easy coffee table.

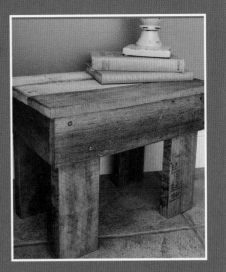

Make four stools 11" or shorter to fit under the coffee table (page 52). They are perfect for kids to sit on and provide extra seating or footrests when you have company.

Two or three stools stacked on top of each other make a simple side table.

I like to use stools as decoration. Place them in an empty corner to add a little color and a place to set a few decorative items.

Step stools help to add height to displays. Try one on your kitchen table as part of a centerpiece.

BENCH

A good, solid bench can be used in so many different parts of the home. In the entryway, it's a convenient place to sit while removing or putting on shoes. A bench provides seating at the kitchen table, looks lovely holding extra pillows and blankets at the foot of a bed, and is a wonderful addition to the garden. A bench also can do double duty as a narrow coffee table in small spaces. This pallet bench can be personalized in many different ways to fit your home and decor. Where will you use this versatile bench?

SUPPLIES

- One pallet with wide spaces between slats (My pallet is 40" × 48".)
- Three 2" × 4" pallet boards, at least 48" long
- Eight to ten pallet boards the same thickness as the boards on the pallet and that fit in the open slats (I used 3½"-wide boards.)
- 2" screws
- 1⅝" screws
- Paint (I used Fusion Mineral Paint, color Ceramic.)
- Paintbrushes
- Stain
- Clear sealer

TOOLS

- Saw
- Palm sander
- Drill
- Tape measure
- Clamps
- Pencil

TIME: 1½ hours, plus dry time   LEVEL: Intermediate

1 Remove the back support boards from the pallet.

2 Draw a straight line down the middle of the pallet, just to the side of the center middle board. Following the line, saw the pallet in half, leaving the middle and one side 2" × 4" board on the half you will use as the bench top.

3 Measure the distance on the open ends of the bench between the two long sides. On this bench, the measurement is 17½".

4 Cut two 2" × 4" pallet boards the length you measured, and attach them with 2" screws inserted from the long sides of the bench.

5 Measure the length of the top pallet boards (mine are 21" long) and the width of the open spaces (mine are 3½" wide). Cut enough pallet boards to fit in the open spaces. Expect some boards to fit snuggly and some to have a little space between them. You can sand the edges of some of the boards to help them fit the open spaces better.

6 Secure the pallet boards in the open spaces with 1⅝" screws, using two screws in each board end.

7 Using 2" × 4" pallet boards, cut four 16" long pieces for legs. Hold each leg in place with a small clamp, and attach with four 2" screws, two on either side of the leg through the bench sides.

8 Measure the distance between the legs on each side of the bench. Take your measurement near the bench top. It is important to measure at the top of the legs and not near the bottom because the legs may not be square.

9 Cut two 2" × 4" boards the length you measured for cross braces.

10 Mark 4" from the bottom of each leg. This is where you will attach the cross braces.

11 Use a large clamp to hold each cross brace in place. Attach each cross brace with two 2" screws on either side, screwing through the outside of each leg into the brace end.

12 Finish the bench as desired. I chose to paint the apron of the bench and the legs, distress the paint, and then stain the whole bench and then finish with a clear sealer.

PALLET POINTERS: OTHER FINISH IDEAS

Paint the bench top, and stain the apron and legs.

Paint the bench slats different colors, and stain the legs. Use a random pattern rather than a repeating one when painting.

You can't go wrong painting the bench a single color or just staining the bare wood.

Use different colors of stain on different parts of the bench. Chose colors from very light, such as pine, to very dark, like walnut.

Make sure to use a clear sealer intended for outdoor use if you plan on using the bench outdoors. There are several different types available in both a spray-on and a brush-on sealer.

PET BED

Pets, oh, how they love to try and claim the entire house as their own! This is one project that your pooch or kitty-cat will love to claim, and you will be thrilled that the family pet has his or her very own place to sleep. The bonus with this pet bed is that it is on wheels, making it easy to move from room to room, depending on you and your pet's needs. This bed is 18" × 25", ideal for a small- to medium-sized pet, but you can adjust the size of the bed and use a queen- or king-sized pillow and pillowcase to accommodate a larger pet.

SUPPLIES

- Two thick 5½"-wide pallet boards, cut 18" long
- One thick 5½"-wide pallet board, cut 25" long
- One 3½"-wide pallet board, cut 25" long
- Pallet boards in various widths but the same thickness, cut 18" long
- 1⅝" screws
- 1¼" screws
- ¾" screws
- Standard-sized pillow and pillowcase
- Four 2" swivel casters
- Paint
- Paintbrush

TOOLS

- Saw
- Palm sander
- Drill
- Tape measure

TIME: 1½ hours, plus dry time   LEVEL: Intermediate

1 Cut and sand the pallet boards. Sand well so your pet won't get slivers.

2 Make a rectangular frame, using the three 5½"-wide boards for the back and sides of the bed, and the one 3½"-wide board for the front of the bed. Use two 1⅝" screws to secure each of the corners.

3 Turn the bed frame upside down, and add the 18"-long boards to create the bottom of the bed. Arrange the different widths to fit the space. A small space (½" or less) between boards is okay.

4 Attach the bottom boards to the front and back sides with 1⅝" screws.

5 Paint as desired. I painted mine with white enamel latex paint because it wears well and cleans easily.

6 When the paint is dry, add the casters. If your pet is very active, you may want to consider two locking casters on the front of the bed. Use 1¼" screws in the three caster base holes that sit or are placed on the pet bed sides or edges. Use a ¾" screw on the caster base hole that is on the bed bottom so that it does not go through the wood into the bed bottom where your pet will be lying.

7 Decorate the bed frame as desired. I hand-painted "good dog" on the front of the bed. You could add your pet's name or another sentiment that suits your pet.

8 Add a pillow to make the bed soft and comfortable. If your pet likes to tear up stuffed items such as pillows, hand-stitch or machine sew the end of the pillowcase closed.

WINE BAR

Whether you are a wine connoisseur or just enjoy an occasional glass, this wine bar is a perfect addition to any family room or dining room. In addition to working well as a storage piece, it is a classy way to serve your guests. The shelves are slightly tilted to store wine at the proper angle. There is also space to store other beverages, and to hang wine glasses and other stem glasses.

SUPPLIES

- One pallet with boards 40" long

- One large pallet (mine is 36" x 40"), with small enough spaces between pallet boards so that wine bottles will rest on them and not fall through (The boards on mine are approximately 2¼" apart.)

- Four 2" × 4" pallet support boards without notches, at least 40" long

- Two notched 2" × 4" pallet boards, at least 48" long

- Two 3½"-wide pallet boards, 40" long

- Three 5½"-wide pallet boards, at least 32" long
- Pallet boards in various widths but the same thickness, cut 16" long
- 8"-long piece of leather belt
- 2" screws
- 1⅝" screws
- 1¼" screws
- 1⅜" brad nails
- Stain
- Paintbrush
- 8"-long leather belt

TOOLS
- Saw
- Palm sander
- Brad nailer
- Drill
- Tape measure
- Pencil

TIME: 4 hours, plus dry time   LEVEL: Expert

Use the diagram below to help identify the different parts of the wine bar while building it:

WINE BAR TOP
NOTCHED 2" X 4" TOP BRACE
WINE GLASS HOLDERS OR BRACKETS
WINE BAR SIDE
3½" BOARD TO TILT SHELF
WINE BAR SIDE 2" X 4"
WINE SHELVES

1 To make the sections for the sides of the wine bar, saw the pallet with 40" long boards into two sections. Saw through the three 2" × 4" back support boards (two of the 2" × 4" boards run along the sides of the pallet and one runs down the middle). It does not matter on these side pieces if the 2" x 4"s are notched or not. The ones shown are notched.

2 These sections for the sides of the wine bar should be at least 16" wide. I cut mine so that each side has three pallet boards running lengthwise or vertically. The 2" × 4" support boards that hold the pallet together will become the wine shelf braces or brackets.

3 Using the large pallet with small spaces between the boards, measure 16" from each outside edge or outside 2" × 4" and draw a cutting line. You will be cutting each side off or away from the middle 2" × 4" support board.

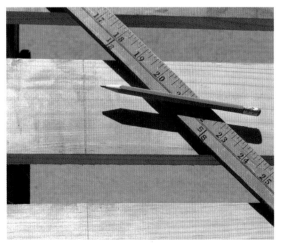

4 Using a saw, cut the pallet boards on the line to make two wine shelves that are 16" wide and 40" long.

5 Cut two 2" × 4" un-notched pallet boards 42" long.

6 Attach the 2" × 4" boards to the wine shelves you created in step 4 with 1¼" screws, one per board, screwing through the bottom of each slat or board.

7 To temporarily connect the two sides of the wine bar, use the wine shelves by setting them in place on the 2" × 4" supports in the middle and at the bottom of the wine bar sides to get the sides properly spaced apart. Push the wine shelves forward 4" and place the 3½" × 40" boards across the middle and bottom side 2" × 4" shelf brace boards (the same boards the wine shelves are on). Use 1⅝" screws to attach the 3½" boards to the supports. The back of the wine shelves will rest on top of the 3½" boards and will create the tilt needed to keep the wine cork moist when the wine bottle is on the shelf.

8 Place the wine shelves with the 2" × 4" boards facing up on top of the 3½" board. Use 1⅝" screws to secure the shelves to the 2" × 4" boards on the sides of the wine bar. The shelves rest on the middle and bottom 2" × 4" pallet braces and on the 3½" wide boards you added in step 7. Remember, because the shelves are resting on the 3½" pallet boards, they will have a slight tilt. This is for proper wine storage—the wine bottle is tilted so the wine keeps the cork moist.

9 To stabilize the shelves, screw two 2" screws on each side through the shelf sides into the 2" × 4" boards on the wine shelves.

10 Place the two 48"-long notched 2" × 4" support boards across the top of the wine bar. Insert three 2" screws through these notched 2" × 4" boards into the top 2" × 4" brace on the wine bar sides to make the wine bar top apron.

11 To make the wine glass holders, cut the 5½"-wide pallet boards into six 16"-long pieces and the straight 2" × 4" boards into five 16" long pieces. Sand the boards. At this point, you may want to stain or finish these boards as desired because it is easier to do it now than when the glass holders are assembled.

12 Turn the wine bar upside down to attach the wine glass holders to the underside of the notched 2" × 4" wine bar top braces. Place the 16" long 2" × 4" boards (cut in step 11) approximately 3½" apart. One 2" × 4" board will end up right next to the 2" × 4" board on the side of the wine bar. This is where a towel holder will go. Center the 5½" × 16" pallet boards on top of the 2" × 4" boards. Do not center the 5½" boards on the two end 2" × 4" boards. These 5½" boards will be flush on one side of each end 2" × 4" board because you are only making one side of a glass holder on each end.

13 Secure the wine glass holders or brackets to the notched 2" × 4" supports on the top of the wine bar with 2" screws, screwing through both the 5½" board and the 2" x 4" board that creates the glass holder.

14 Arrange the pallet boards that are in a variety of widths but the same thickness and 16" long on the top of the wine bar. (I chose different types of wood so that they would stain different colors.) Use a brad nailer and 1⅜" brad nails to attach the boards to the notched braces at the top of the wine bar.

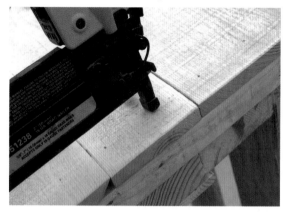

15 Sand and finish the wine bar as desired.

16 Use an 8"-long piece of leather belt to create a towel holder. Attach it to the wine bar with 1¼" screws. You could use a metal utility handle or a coat hook instead, but I like the leather piece because it is soft and does not poke anyone standing at the bar.

THE GREAT OUTDOORS

LAWN TIC-TAC-TOE

This oversized game is fun for both kids and adults, and perfect for family gatherings and summer barbecues. An easy pallet project, it will get your family out of the house and playing together in no time.

SUPPLIES

- Four 3½" × 36" pallet boards
- Two 5½"-wide pallet boards
- 1¼" screws
- Paint
- Paintbrushes
- Stencils (optional)
- Clear sealer

TOOLS

- Saw
- Palm sander
- Drill
- Tape measure

TIME: 1 hour, plus dry time   LEVEL: Beginner

1 Sand the 3½" boards thoroughly, and lay them out in a tic-tac-toe grid. Use two 1¼" screws to secure the boards at each point where they cross.

2 Cut the 5½" pallet boards into ten 5½" squares, and sand them.

3 Paint five of the squares one color, and paint the other five a different color. Stencil or hand-paint Xs and Os in bright white on the squares. Paint the tic-tac-toe grid as well.

4 Seal the grid and squares with a clear sealer intended for outdoor use.

PORCH STAR

A decorated porch and front door is a wonderful way to welcome guests to your home. This star looks great not only for holidays like Christmas and the Fourth of July, but also year-round. It is a quick and simple project that adds impact to a home's exterior.

SUPPLIES

- Five 3½" × 32" pallet boards
- 1¼" screws
- ¾" screws
- Paint
- Paintbrush
- Clear sealer
- Picture hanging wire

TOOLS

- Palm sander
- Drill

TIME: 30 minutes, plus dry time   **LEVEL:** Beginner

1 Place the five boards face down in a star shape.

2 Use 1¼" screws to screw the star together from the back at the points where the boards cross. You may need to add a few screws from the front to further solidify the star.

3 Sand and paint the star as desired. Because this is a decorative piece that will be hanging on a wall and not touched, a light sanding is all that is needed. Apply a clear sealer intended for outdoors use.

4 Use two ¾" screws to attach picture hanging wire on the back of the star.

PALLET POINTERS: VARIATIONS

Make stars in different sizes and display them as a trio.

Instead of using one color, paint each board a different color, and do it before assembling the star.

Wrap twinkle lights around the star to light it at night.

A star also makes a great indoor decoration—try it above a fireplace.

POTTING BENCH

Whether you are a hardcore gardener growing your own vegetables and herbs or you just like to have a few colorful flowers in pots on your front steps, a potting bench will simplify your work. It gives you a place to organize and store your gardening supplies, as well as space to work on your potted plants while standing up — which is much easier on your back than bending to the ground.

SUPPLIES

- One pallet with large spaces between pallet boards (this one is 36" × 36")

- Five 2" × 4" pallet boards

- Four 3½"-wide pallet boards, at least 36" long

- One 3½"-wide to 4"-wide pallet board, at least 40" long

- One 5½"-wide (or wider) pallet board, at least 36" long

- Pallet boards in a width (generally 3½" or narrower) that will fit in the large spaces in main pallet
- 2" screws
- 1⅝" screws
- 1¼" screws
- 1⅜" brad nails
- Hooks
- Paint in various colors
- Paintbrushes
- Clear sealer

TOOLS

- Saw
- Palm sander
- Drill
- Brad nailer
- Tape measure
- Clamps

TIME: 3 hours, plus dry time   LEVEL: Expert

1 Saw the pallet in half along the center 2" × 4" support board, leaving the 2" × 4" attached to the side of the pallet that will become the potting bench top.

2 Measure the end width of the potting bench top. Cut two 3½"- to 4"-wide pallet boards this length. The end pictured here is 18¾" long.

3 Attach the boards to the potting bench top ends with 1⅝" screws.

POTTING BENCH TOP
POTTING BENCH BACK

4 Cut four 2" × 4" pallet boards 36" long for the legs. With the potting bench turned upside down, clamp the legs in place, and insert two 2" screws into the front and two 2" screws into the side of the potting bench apron to secure each leg.

5 The other half of the pallet will form the upright back of the potting bench. Secure the back with 1⅝" screws, two per pallet board, securing the two end or outside pieces first. I was able to hold the back section in place with one hand and drill with the other, but you can use clamps if needed.

6 At this point I stained the potting bench. It is not necessary to do it now, but it is a little easier to get the stain in all the nooks and crannies if you do.

7 Measure the top 2" × 4" board on the pallet back. Cut the 5½"-wide pallet board this length (36" long in the case of the potting bench pictured here).

8 To determine the length for the bottom shelf brackets, measure the distance between the outside edges of the legs at the top of the bench near the apron. It is important to measure at the top of the legs and not near the bottom because the legs may not be square. The shelf brackets will help to square up the legs and make the potting bench sturdier. Cut two 2" × 4" pieces the length you measured (16¼" long for this potting bench).

9 Measure the length between the inside edges of the legs, across the front of the bench. Cut four 3½"-wide pallet boards this length (29" long for the potting bench pictured here).

10 Measure the length of the pallet boards that form the top of the potting bench. Cut the pallet boards of various widths the same length you just measured, and make sure the boards will fit in the spaces. I needed to sand the edges of some cut boards to get them to fit.

11 Paint and stain all of the boards you took measurements for and cut in steps 7, 8, 9, and 10. I did not paint the 2" × 4" shelf brackets.

12 Measure and mark 11" from the bottom of each leg.

13 Place the top edge of the shelf brackets on the 11" mark. Using 2" screws, attach the shelf brackets to the legs, making sure the edges of the brackets are flush with the edges of the legs.

14 Evenly place the 3½" wide boards you cut in Step 9 on the shelf brackets. Attach the pallet boards to the brackets with 1¼" screws.

15 Create a top shelf by attaching the 5½"-wide (or wider) pallet board you cut in Step 7 to the 2" × 4" board at the top of the potting bench back. Secure with 1¼" screws.

16 Fit the pallet boards you cut in Step 10 into the spaces on the potting bench top, and secure with a brad nailer and 1⅜" brads. You could use 1¼" screws instead.

17 Accessorize your potting bench with hooks for garden tools, gloves, towels, and a bottle opener.

18 Finish and protect the potting bench with a clear sealer made for outdoor use.

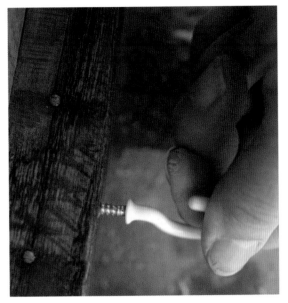

This piece can serve double duty as a potting bench and a buffet for barbecues and get-togethers. Be sure to add a bottle opener so you can have a refreshing drink when gardening and guests can help themselves to beverages at outdoor parties. The bench doesn't have to go outdoors if you have more use for it indoors — it looks great in a kitchen or entryway.

ART AND DECOR

GALLERY WALL

What is a gallery wall? It is a collection or grouping of items on a wall that has a common theme and typically includes family photos. These three fun and easy pallet projects work well together to add color and personality to any blank wall.

ARROW SUPPLIES

- Three 3½" × 40" pallet boards
- One 90-degree triangle cut from a 5½"-wide pallet board
- Paint in various colors
- Paintbrushes
- One metal 4" flat joining plate
- 1" screws
- Wood glue
- Clear sealer
- Picture hanging wire

TOOLS

- Saw
- Miter saw or miter box
- Palm sander
- Drill
- Tape measure

TIME: 30 minutes, plus dry time   LEVEL: Beginner

1 Cut two of the 3½" × 40" boards 24" long. Keep the extra 16" scrap pieces.

2 Place the 90-degree triangle next to one of the 3½"-wide scrap boards. Mark the wide side of the triangle on the board.

3 Place the triangle at the mark and trace the angle. Cut using the miter saw or miter box. You will make a trapezoid shape.

4 From the remaining 16" scrap and the 3½" x 40" board, using the miter saw, cut four 3½" × 10" parallelograms with 45-degree angles. These will form the arrow tailpieces.

5 Paint the individual pieces before assembling them. I used a combination of light blues, greens, and turquoises.

6 Join the 24"-long boards with the metal plate and 1" screws to form the body of the arrow.

7 Make the arrow tip by using a 3½" × 3½" square to join the triangle and the trapezoid.

8 Connect the tip to the arrow body with 1" screws through the backs of the pieces.

9 Using wood glue, secure the arrow tailpieces. Use something heavy like a container of screws to weight them. When the glue is dry, secure the tailpieces with 1" screws inserted through the back.

10 Sand and seal the arrow. Use two 1" screws to attach picture hanging wire on the back of the arrow.

FAMILY SIGN SUPPLIES

- Four pallet boards in various widths, cut 22" long
- Two pallet boards cut to the height of the sign (mine is 18" tall)
- 1" screws
- Chalk
- Paint
- Paintbrush
- Stain
- Picture hanging wire

TOOLS

- Saw
- Palm sander
- Drill
- Tape measure

TIME: 30 minutes, plus dry time   LEVEL: Beginner

1 Choose the boards you want to use for the sign and lay them face down. Place the joiner boards, cut to the height of the sign (18" for this sign), across the back.

2 Use 1" screws to join the sign. Insert two screws into each board at an angle to secure the sign.

3 Write your chosen sentiment in chalk on the sign. (See Pallet Pointers: Sign Lettering on page 96).

4 Paint your letters using white semi-gloss latex paint. I use semi-gloss paint whenever I will be staining over lettering because stain does not stick to semi-gloss and so the lettering stays white.

5 Lightly sand the sign, and stain it.

6 Use two 1" screws to attach picture hanging wire to the back of the sign.

PICTURE HOLDER SUPPLIES

- Two 5½" × 33½" pallet boards
- Four 3½" × 11" pallet boards
- Paint in various colors
- Stain
- Paintbrushes
- 1" screws
- Picture hanging wire

TOOLS

- Palm sander
- Drill
- Tape measure

TIME: 30 minutes, plus dry time   LEVEL: Beginner

1 Paint the 5½"-wide boards (I painted one green and the other turquoise). Once the boards are dry, place them side by side, face down on top of a horizontal 11" pallet board. The 11" pallet board should line up with the top ends of the painted boards. Secure with two 1" screws per painted board.

2 Measure 6¾" down from the bottom of the 11" board that is across the top, and mark on each side of the painted boards. Secure another 11" cross board here. Do not screw tightly — you need to slip pictures under the cross boards. Repeat for the remaining two 11" boards.

3 Sand the assembled picture holder, and stain it.

4 Use two 1" screws to attach picture hanging wire to the back.

5 Tuck 5" × 7" photos under the cross boards. If they slip too far under the cross boards, tighten the screws in the back.

PALLET POINTERS: SIGN LETTERING

There are several ways to letter signs.

I usually hand-letter most of my signs. The best way to get the letters just right is to use white chalk to sketch letters as a guide.

Stencils purchased from a craft store give you neater, more precise lettering. Use a chalk line to keep the lettering straight.

Vinyl letters cut from machines also produce neat lettering.

You can easily make your own stencil with your computer. Print the text you want and rub white chalk over the back of the paper. Tape the paper on the sign and trace over the letters with a blunt pencil tip. When you remove the paper, you'll see the outline of chalk where you traced with the pencil. Paint the letters by hand. This technique takes a little more time, but the font possibilities are endless.

ABSTRACT, INSPIRATIONAL WORD ART

Finding items to fill your walls at an affordable price can be a challenge. More than just budget-friendly art, I want things that are unique and personal to my family and me. On top of that, I want to change the decor as the seasons or whim hits me. This wall art fits the bill perfectly and can be personalized in many different ways. It is a very quick project that uses up bits and pieces of pallet wood from other projects.

SUPPLIES

- Pallet boards in various widths, thicknesses, and lengths
- Paint in various colors
- Semi-gloss white paint
- Stain
- Paintbrushes
- Chalk
- 1" screws
- Picture-hanging wire

TOOLS

- Saw
- Palm sander
- Drill

TIME: 1 hour, plus dry time   LEVEL: Beginner

1 Gather and cut a variety of pallet boards, including some long or full-length boards. Paint as desired, or use boards you previously painted. Make sure the boards are sanded well before assembling them because it is difficult to sand some of them after they are put together.

2 Arrange the boards as desired, placing them over and under each other. Choose any size and shape you like, and arrange the boards accordingly.

3 Join the boards with 1" screws inserted through the back. Use two screws when joining each board and place them at an angle.

4 Using chalk, write inspirational words that are meaningful to you.

5 Paint over the chalked words with semi-gloss white paint, using a small brush.

6 If you want a more weathered look, stain the entire piece as directed on page 13.

7 Use two 1" screws to attach picture-hanging wire stretched across one of the horizontal boards. Cut a long piece of wire so you can find the correct point of balance when hanging the art.

PALLET POINTERS: PERSONALIZING

Use this technique to create a decorative family tree. Write your family name on one of the main boards, and then add individual names and birthdates on the surrounding boards.

Screw binder clips to the boards to make a fun photo display.

Add coat hooks to the boards, and hang the artwork in an entryway.

Make a holiday decoration by using colors and words relating to the holiday.

Record details about a baby's birth—length, weight, time of birth—for a unique nursery decoration.

BLANKET DISPLAY LADDER

I love furniture that is not only decorative but also functional. This quick and easy project can be used to hold blankets in a bedroom or towels in a bathroom. It fits a small space and is a great way to add height to displays. I made this ladder extra tall — 8 feet — but you can adjust the height to suit your needs. Caution: This ladder is for display only and not for climbing.

SUPPLIES

- Four 2" × 4" pallet support boards, cut 4' long, notched or straight
- Two pallet board scrap squares, 3½" × 3½"
- Seven pallet boards cut 14" long (I use different width boards because I like the primitive look of the different widths.)
- 1⅝" screws
- 1¼" screws
- Paint
- Clear sealer
- Paintbrush

TOOLS

- Palm sander
- Drill
- Tape measure

1 Lightly sand all boards before assembly. The rungs (14"-long boards) should be especially smooth since they will hold blankets.

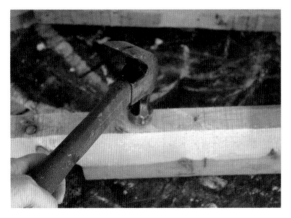

2 Hammer down any cut nails that protrude on the 2" × 4" boards.

3 Join the 2" × 4" pallet support boards with one of the wider 14" boards. Secure this middle rung with 1⅝" screws.

4 Use the 3½" scrap squares to secure the 2" × 4" pieces on the inside of the ladder. Screw each square securely in place with 1¼" screws.

5 Measure 10" from the middle rung in either direction, mark, and add another 14" rung, using the 1¼" screws. Continue adding the remaining rungs.

6 Paint as desired and finish with a clear sealer.

PALLET POINTERS: VARIATIONS

Use your display ladder in the kitchen to hang kitchen towels. Add S-shaped hooks to the rungs to hang pots and pans and kitchen utensils.

A smaller version of this ladder, 3 feet tall, used as a trellis for a vining plant makes a great front door or fireplace decoration.

Keep a display ladder near the pool or hot tub to hold towels. Be sure to seal well with a finish intended for outdoor use.

BITS AND PIECES: USING PALLET SCRAPS

TRIVET

The trivet is a must for protecting counters and tabletops from hot dishes. This trivet can be customized to fit any decor, and it's sturdy enough to hold any hot dish.

SUPPLIES

- Six 3½" × 10½" pallet boards
- 1¼" screws
- Roll of cork (from a craft store)
- All-purpose white craft glue
- Clear sealer
- Paintbrush

TOOLS

- Palm sander
- Drill
- Tape measure

TIME: 20 minutes, plus dry time   **LEVEL:** Beginner

1 Sand the pallet boards well. I used three previously painted boards for the top of the trivet and three unpainted boards for the bottom.

2 Turn the painted boards face down, side by side horizontally. Place the unpainted boards on top of the face-down painted boards, side by side vertically. Join the boards with 1¼" screws.

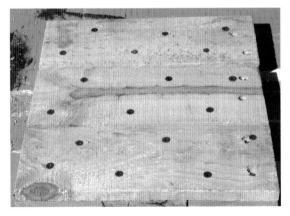

3 Cut a piece of cork the same size as the trivet (10½" × 10½").

4 Apply a heavy coat of white craft glue to the unpainted bottom of the trivet, and position the cork over it. Clean up any drips.

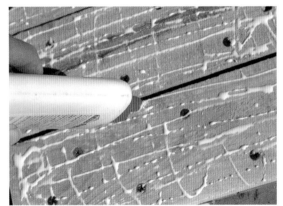

5 Place a flat object that covers the whole trivet, such as a large book, record album, or board, on top of the cork and weigh it with something heavy until the glue is dry.

6 Protect the trivet with a clear sealer applied to the top and sides.

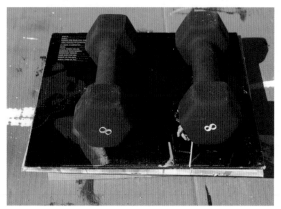

HOUSE NUMBERS

I love keeping all of my colorful pallet scraps and then painting numbers or letters on them. They make fun and unique house numbers, and random numbers and letters also look great just sitting in an interesting bowl on your coffee table.

SUPPLIES
- Small painted pallet scraps
- One pallet board long enough to hold address numbers (mine is 12")
- 1¼" screws
- Paint
- Paintbrush
- Stencils (optional)
- Clear sealer
- D rings

TOOLS
- Palm sander
- Drill

TIME: 20 minutes, plus dry time   LEVEL: Beginner

1 Hand-paint or stencil numbers on small pallet scrap scraps.

2 Turn the scraps with the numbers face down, and place the pallet board over them. Secure the numbers to the pallet board with two 1¼" screws per number.

3 Seal the house numbers with a good sealer intended for outdoor use.

4 Attach D rings to the back of the board to hang the numbers. As an alternative, screw the board directly into the house wall for a more permanent attachment.

MEMORY GAME

Memory games are fun for younger children, and they help to develop important thinking skills. This pallet wood version has pieces that are easy for even the smallest of hands to pick up and turn over. You can choose to make as many memory pairs as you like, but eight pairs is a good number for smaller children.

SUPPLIES
- Sixteen pallet squares, 3½" × 3½"
- Craft paints
- Paintbrushes
- Clear sealer
- Stencils (optional)

TOOLS
- Palm sander

TIME: 45 minutes, plus dry time   LEVEL: Beginner

1 Sand the squares thoroughly.

2 Paint one side of the squares the same color.

3 On the other side of the squares, paint pairs of simple objects like a tree, flower, sun, sailboat, bird, watermelon, and star. As an alternative, you could stencil designs or use stickers or even photos on the squares.

4 Protect both sides of the squares with a clear sealer.

KEY HOLDER

No one likes spending time looking for misplaced keys. Hang this simple key holder near the front door and you will always know where your keys are. It makes a nice housewarming gift for a family or a gift for a teenager getting a driver's license. Project inspired by Angie at knickoftime.net.

SUPPLIES
- One 2" × 4" pallet wood scrap, approximately 10" long
- Paint
- Paintbrush
- Clear sealer
- Chalk
- Three cup hooks
- D rings

TOOLS
- Palm sander
- Drill

TIME: 20 minutes, plus dry time   LEVEL: Beginner

1 Sand the wood scrap. If it isn't already painted, paint as desired.

2 Using chalk, hand draw a skeleton key on the scrap piece. Paint with white paint and seal with a clear sealer.

3 Drill three evenly spaced holes in the bottom edge of the key holder. Screw in 3 cup hooks.

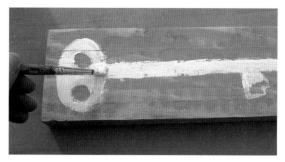

4 Add D rings to the back for hanging.

COASTERS

If you build it, they will come — or how I see it, if you have it, they will use it. If you want your family to use coasters to protect your furniture, you need to have plenty scattered about for them to use. These simple coasters are a breeze to make.

SUPPLIES
- Four pallet squares, 3½" × 3½"
- Roll of cork (from a craft store)
- Paint, if using
- Paintbrush, if using
- All-purpose white craft glue
- Coconut oil
- T-shirt rag

TOOLS
- Saw
- Palm sander

TIME: 20 minutes, plus dry time   LEVEL: Beginner

1 Sand the pallet squares well. Paint or finish as desired. I chose to leave the natural wood.

2 Cut four pieces of cork the same size as each coaster (3½" × 3½"). Liberally apply craft glue to the bottom of each coaster, and position the cork over it. Clean up any drips.

3 Place a large book, record album, or board over all four coasters with the cork side up. Weigh down the coasters with something heavy.

4 Apply two coats of coconut oil with a soft T-shirt rag. Apply one coat and let it soak into the wood for 24 hours before applying the second coat. The oil will protect the wood and repel liquids.

APPENDIX

RESOURCES

COCONUT OIL is an excellent natural finish for indoor projects, like the Coffee Table (page 52) and Coasters (page 113). Coconut oil can be found at most grocery stores; I prefer the Kirkland brand from Costco.

FUNKY JUNK INTERIORS (funkyjunkinteriors.net) offers numerous high-quality stencils that will look great on several of these pallet projects.

FUSION MINERAL PAINT (fusionmineralpaint.com) is a favorite for mineral-based paints like the ones used in the Bench (page 64) and Jewelry Organizer (page 32).

MAKITA (makitatools.com) tools are ideal for any of the projects in this book. They are lightweight and powerful. My favorites are the Makita 18V cordless hammer and rotary drill. They can be purchased online or at hardware stores such as Lowe's or Home Depot.

MINWAX (minwax.com) stains were used on all stained projects. Tips and colors can be found at their website.

RUSTIC IRON STORE (rusticironstore.com) sells a fantastic variety of handles and hooks at a low price, great for projects like the Towel Holder (page 48).

METRIC CONVERSIONS

U.S. UNIT	METRIC
¼ inch	6.35 millimeters
½ inch	12.7 millimeters
¾ inch	1.905 centimeters
1 inch	2.54 centimeters
1 foot (12 inches)	.3048 meter
1 yard (3 feet)	.9144 meter

INDEX

ACKNOWLEDGMENTS

My name may be listed as the author, but without the help, support, and encouragement of many, this book would not have been written. To my husband, Paul: Your brain works in a completely different way from mine, but you still patiently work alongside me, helping me when needed and letting me figure it out on my own when needed. Thank you. You are the best pallet spotter and hauler I know. To my children, Tate, Keldon, and Tessa: Thank you for letting me test out my ideas and projects on you, and for graciously putting up with paint and projects all over the house, missed meals, and endless pallet wood piles. Thank you Carolyn Slayden, my mom. You motivated me to create with what I could find and what was in the budget and taught me that I can do it myself. To my sister, Karen Washut, and friend Rachel Pierson: Thank you for cheering me on and encouraging me to keep plugging along even when it was a challenge. To Missy Severson and the gang at The Antique Barn: Your enthusiasm and laughter lighten the workload and brighten the day. Thank you Tina Beckman, my business partner in selling our crazy creations: Your creativity and building skills push me to be better. And finally, thank you to Casie Vogel, my editor, for finding me, for holding my hand and reassuring me throughout the book-writing process.

ABOUT THE AUTHOR

BECKY LAMB is a builder, junker, repurposer, blogger, crafter, teacher, wife, and mother of three. Her work has been featured in *Country Home* and *GreenCraft Magazine* and on the television show *Home and Family*. Becky has been crafting and creating as long as she can remember and discovered her love for building in 2000, when she started to sell home decor items at local shows and markets. In 2008, she started writing about and sharing her building and creating adventures on her blog, Beyond the Picket Fence. When not building, Becky enjoys spending time outdoors with her family in her home state of Montana.